Restricted View

Olivia Cole is an award-winning poet and journalist, writing for the *Spectator* and the *London Evening Standard*. She specialises in the arts, literature and London's party scene. Olivia was born in 1981 in Kent, and read English at Christ Church, Oxford. *Restricted View* is her first poetry collection. In 2003 she won an Eric Gregory award, the Society of Authors' awards for poets under the age of 30.

Restricted View

OLIVIA COLE

SALT

LONDON

PUBLISHED BY SALT PUBLISHING
Fourth Floor, 2 Tavistock Place, Bloomsbury, London WC1H 9RA United Kingdom

© Olivia Cole, 2009

Salt Publishing 2009

Printed in Great Britain by the MPG Books Group, Bodmin and King's Lynn

Typeset in Swift 9.5 / 13

ISBN 978 1 84471 569 5 paperback

1 3 5 7 9 8 6 4 2

For my parents

Contents

Acknowledgements

Thanks to the editors of the following publications where some of these poems first appeared : *Magma*, *The Wolf*, *The Liberal*, the *London Evening Standard* and the *Independent on Sunday*. Some of these poems also appeared in the anthologies *Ask For It By Name* (London 2008) *Tower Poets* (Oxford 2005) and *Promises to Keep* (London 2003). 'Il Duce's Match' was the winner of the 2003 writers inc prize. Thanks are also due to the Society of Authors and the 2003 judges of the Eric Gregory awards, and to Arvon and the Jerwood Foundation, who 'apprenticed' me in 2003 to Christopher Reid whose continuing wise mentoring is very much appreciated. For their inspiration and encouragement, I am indebted also to Clive James, Chris Greenhalgh, Anthony Theaker, Richard and Imogen Barker, Christopher Butler, Peter Conrad, Peter McDonald, Craig Raine, Hugo Williams and the late Michael Donaghy. For reading these poems in their earliest forms, thank you too, to all of my City contemporaries. For their conviction that poet/journalist isn't an oxymoron, my thanks are also due to Sebastian Shakespeare, Geordie Greig and Matthew d'Ancona. Thanks also go to Dave Benett, Anouschka Menzies, Eliot Sandiford, to Chris Hamilton-Emery for making this book happen, and to Natasha Archdale for creating the perfect 'restricted view' of a writer. My grandparents, Eileen and Cyril Howard, aren't here to see this book in its finished form, but I wish that they were, and know that they would have been very proud. For thinking that a teenager who thought a power cut was a good chance to read poetry by candlelight was to be encouraged, love and thanks to Mummy, Daddy, Georgina and Harry Cole and to Richard Hains, for thinking that it's a nonsense that happiness writes white . . .

Then Adam became Mr Chatterbox . . . arguing that people did not really mind *whom* they read about provided that a kind of vicarious inquisitiveness into the lives of others was satisfied, Adam began to invent people.

EVELYN WAUGH, *Vile Bodies*

Breaking the Ice

A metallic aftertaste, a gild,
a shine, right or wrong, a glint
of something strong; feet on frost,
an awkwardness that makes
every crunched word loud, every glance
a look; an aperitif cold as arrogance
or a cruel streak. One day we could wake
to a better, warmer kind of gleam

that we'll love more than this askance rude stutter.
And we'll drink deep but knowing all the while
that it tastes nothing like this first stop start
glitter that once gone—twisted, bitter—
there's no way we can demand again,
at least not here and now, with each other.

Between Some Acts

In the Piazza Bra, Verona

Victor Emmanuel looks on at the gathering dusk
and crowd. Cast in iron he must be used, by now,
to this purpose in the air, to this sweep of pale sky—
when next I looked away from the arena's stage,
I found it dark. For each act the moon climbed higher.

Sporadic stars disappeared and reappeared through cloud
and bats or tiny birds in phosphorescent free fall, too small to see,
flickered—held, in the spotlight's beam. Moving
to track Carmen, as gently and intently as a lover,
it caught them too, their dark mechanics of flight,

suspended, beating, stagecraft exposed above
the candles and the crowd. All night they hovered before
that paper world, its painted dusk, and cigarette girls,
and later, with real light and another night not far away
she swept, alive, in a haze of bouquets and friends

past the square's cafes—her tiny puppet figure,
pin-holed, near, magnified to laughter, conversation, dawn,
cold wine, the lighting of another and another
cigarette. Unwound now, free for a few hours
till she wakes so late in the day—to the rustle

of cellophane, once more, and feels the day's heat rise
against the shutters, the hours, the wilting flowers.
Body taut as a lizard, her lips mouth lines.
Already in the wings she remembers how the light
must fade, and fearful as a lazy tourist, she waits

to make a break from shade, chased out into brightness.

Balcony Scene

Far below, a boy skating, dangerously close
to the solid jump of the curb. The hard cycles
of the wheels rolling over and over themselves
as I gaze. A ladybird, precariously high,

on the cool white stone, leaping to pause
on my arm's bared skin before I flick it
unthinkingly: the building falling gently away.
The sun, soon to lie low in the sky,

content for now, to be squinted into,
sharpening the worn silver of my ring
to a glassy, newly moulded tint; a man
and a woman grounded in a conversation

I can't hope to hear, cartoon gestures,
heated words lost to the warm air,
and cars whose paths my eyes lazily trace,
until they disappear from view.

Common Ground

When we're awkward, upset, unsure,
you retreat into travelled, lived out musing,
eloquence in another place or time or mood
intriguing. I'll listen, walking amongst
the daylight couples and dogs and kids
and the traffic's not so distant roar,
and smile and want to cry, and wait,
for that moment when I can't not speak.

And now you know the rules of this game
we've played before, how suddenly
the words will float, slow motion sneezes
on a crowded bus or tube, how your face must
turn, guarded, attempting open and concerned,
do you wait, confident it will come, as it must
with the faint pulse of the winter sun retreating,
or are you content to let this pause go on and on.

Restricted View

For Martin Amis

Cast yourself into a chair, excuse your limbs,
feet, shoes, as they find a path around and over
the legs of those who sit in a row,

gathered to wait for the writer who takes
the stage with assured caution, *tiny, nervous,
practised* steps, to speak, between thought

and the lighting of a cigarette, unconsciously
of the writer's unconscious fear—unable to do
anything but let slip through the blue, a flitter

of anxiety, as he tells of how, 'the life's not the
romantic cutting off of one's ear' and tenderly
strokes his own—still there—visible through

the pauses that load the swirling air.

Bathers At Asnières

After Seurat

Move in too close and this world could fall
apart—sit far enough away and let weekenders
float by, adding girls and wives to the stolen
Monday leisure of basking men and boys.

Let you and I remain convinced of the chase
and flirt of two punts, their slow dance, and
close call, of book and newspaper being read,
let the leather of boots seem hard enough, from here,

for walking. Forget the hand and eye of the puppeteer
who, sketch book and models abandoned somewhere
near Asnières, found the true false suppleness
of a girl in a pool, convinced that like a ballerina she

can stretch and fly, the ease and arrogance of weightlessness
letting him cast by once more from the other side
of the decade, world and river: re-finding a boy's hat
as red, and pencilling out the discarded clothes of lovers.

Flight Paths

I stood in your shower, how many times?
Well, so many times, pausing always
to look through steam and water and glass
at the city's ineradicable stretch,

washing, wondering how many there must be
to give that flickering orange haze
of glimpsed specifics—rooms, yellow
and stacked, curtains raised to show

silhouettes walking across *their* sets,
drawing, eating, murdering quietly
for all I know or could do—
glances, pauses, halves

of dancing couples illuminated,
until they slip from view to pursue
the routes that have for them,
like us, become routine; their shadow play

hanging on the flick of a single switch,
goodbyes played out elaborately across the hours—
as I would stand, one tentative fingertip
tracking across the centimeters and the miles,

the city a condensed pane of glass
to reach for and write on—traced and known:
as impossible to hold as remembered strings of amber beads,
glinting un-lifted from long passed market stalls.

Matinee Idol

I was seventeen, *you're joking? Christ alive,*
and you with all the worldliness
that comes of playing everyone,
were twenty eight or was it nine?

Remember Stratford's river lights,
strings of unlucky lucky pearls, the Dirty Duck,
and some other bar, red—a womb you said.
Remember *darlin'*, how later,

in someone's rhododendron garden,
Mozart floated by candlelight over houses
and up to stars—you found us wine
and damp sun beds to sit whispering on,

until words slowed and eye to eye
my head was in your hands, my mouth
on yours; the empty theatre lying dark and low
on a tide that flowed all the way to winter.

Persistence

The night air sharp against my cheek:
a garden and its party. Strings
of coloured lights pick out faces—
pink and blue grotesques, strangers,

glasses of green and blue liquid
raised to lurid lips, as I smile and shiver
and try to find your eyes. Later, thoughts think
of settling into sleep, my window wide

onto the street, close to water, black and limpid
as milk by day, just a sliver of silver
through the trees—the fountains,
delicately wet, splitting their shadow,

the sculpture they build and break:
again and again through the night,
the sound of water on water,
strange and almost familiar now.

A to Z

Just there in the park
is where we used to lie
and burn. The sun,
flecks of gold in your hair,
your head heavy in my lap,

face open to the sky,
eyes closed in a slow blink
that missed me
squinting to read you
like a timetable or map.

The Cure for Love
After Baudelaire, The Perfume Bottle

Don't think I'd know the name,
duty free, or on the back of someone
else's bathroom shelf, but just once in a while,
your aftershave (mixed with washing powder,
laced with smoke) catches my throat; can turn

ice to glass, a pane that dissolves:
this close up of a lover, a face never mine
to keep or own but even so the screen
starts to flicker with the same few tired scenes.
A cracked bottle rolls on the street.

There's no message inside, no
crowd to see thoughts that should lie low
open up and flower: pink and gold
stargazing lilies, they take off too fast, leaving me
standing still, travel sick. I shut my eyes

inhale again but the deft, fake trace has gone.
I blush obvious as a doodle: felt pen,
initials, roses, straight to the point, arrows
that don't prevaricate, red as the lit tip
of your cigarette that, go on, would burn

right through this paper heart I've sent to you.

Ponte Sant'Angelo

Rome. Pope Clement IX declared Bernini's angels too lovely to be exposed to the weather. Copies were made for the Ponte Sant'Angelo and the originals remained with Bernini's family until 1729, when they were moved to a church. (Spoken by one of the copies).

I have sisters who live in a church,
dreaming of air, the clinging damp
of low dawn tides. I have sisters, smooth
and white as brides, that the pope
couldn't bear to let outside. In the sun,
in the wind or the rain, grey as a ghost
and moulded green, I look my age
and watch you walk away. Don't tell me

you don't love them more, but even so,
deep down, come on, you know it's true—
they are, what can I say? Too *good* for you.
Get off the floor. I know it's me,
out here, who makes you shiver.
I've seen the way you cross and re-cross the river.

The Bridal Suite

Eleanor de Toledo's rooms, Palazzo Vecchio, Florence.
(Eleanor de Toledo was the child bride of Cosimo de Medici)

Camera Verde—two plaster cupids draw
the curtains back—note the knowing look
on the face of one. A moon, of all
the mad chaste things to paint on my wall,

circling the earth, an assigned path,
serving also as a pearl, waiting always
to fall almost without sound into the waiting
cup, while I and the world can only watch.

When Vasari and Bronzino have rolled
up their plans, white spirited their brushes
and moved elsewhere *you will live here*,
walk between these walls, sleep between

these sheets, now this quarter is complete—
your sphere. Echoes, faint shadows, of stories
and cities—Habsburg home from home,
the idea. *In your, our, honour, my dear.*

These rooms, the world on their walls,
the earth, the moon, opulent perfected
props, part of the stage set, waiting
always for the main event. Look as I

looked, walk as I walked, see the roles
I played, two empires and eagles intertwined,
Sabine woman, quiet diplomat, Penelope.
Love played about and love played at across

counsel table, bedroom and hall. Read of the *Duchess*,
the *eighteen year old bride*, of how I offered
up myself, a child, and a little later—
birds on all the walls freeze framed as free,

in flight and always the right way.
Find for me the ones I never saw completed,
barely there sketches on workshop floors,
alabaster tracings, too late to augur anything,

whilst elsewhere another shadow—faded—
stopped breathing, and slipped out the door.
Exit Sortie Ausgang. Many wait to see
what you have seen. Please move on.

Il Duce's Match

Rome, summer 1940. Mussolini attempted to impress the Americans with his tennis and to retain control by penning every headline printed . . .

Your serve was never great—often out of control,
every other ball would soar so high and plummet
to the ground, whistling as quietly as a bomb,
the fatal one they say you hear or is it never hear . . .

before landing miles out. *Second serve.*
I remember how time after time, I willed it to go right,
for you to push ball over net with the softness
and precision of a kitten, the relief

of those occasional rallies. You small and hot
and reddening, as three turned into four o'clock,
flagging opposite streams of young diplomats—
all important friendships wooed across those warm weeks—

the need for an ally behind your struggle
to entertain the *Yanks*, to master *tennis*:
that summer's most popular and most fashionable
invented game. Our shaded court, the heavy air,

cut by laughter and *fifteen love, il Duce,*
applause on cue. *Net.* The ball splicing over,
as close a call as those I would wake to,
listening from our huge white bed, to you

in the bathroom, as you washed and shaved,
only your shadow visible on the cool of the black marble floor
as I resisted the start of each day—content to lie
and listen to the sound of your beauty regime:

the slow scraping of razor across skin, left to right,
straining to reach the very back of the head
you shaved entirely the day you blushed
to find your hair receding—a soft low curse

as occasionally the razor slipped
and caught flesh, those little red flecks of error
that in all those hundreds of posed pictures never
showed up. *Prediletto*, I think, even now, of how

when time began to run like sand through your hands,
you would wake worrying from the dream
in which you forgot to shave your head,
love fifteen, were late at your desk, and a headline

not penned by you slipped though the net, *love thirty*,
and you couldn't find an umpire to lie, *love forty*,
and make decisions, *thirty love*, at which those lithe American boys
would shake their heads, *forty love*, and frown, *game, set, match*,

and shrug, as I stood by waiting with lemonade, Coca Cola
and Pimms, all the latest, necessary fads,
looking from under my broad rimmed expensive hat,
on their gold tanned flesh . . .

I dream too, of those summer days, and wake convinced
even now of what you—dead, defeated
and gone—said you always knew:
that it's the details—*piccolo, minuscolo*—

that matter most in the end; the seconds
and the split seconds between serves, that shot
that you almost, but not quite, got,
the sun in your eyes, the all important present or absent

breeze in the trees; dreams, in which the world, *amore*,
is not black and white, but colour—
so that the blood shows up—those minute nicks that through
un-remembering sleep, some mornings, I still reach to kiss.

Gossip Column

Hats off
to me, who has fallen
for you.
I've been seen,
holding hands,
looking glassy eyed,
with a big grin on my face.
Close to my
West London home,
I've been spotted, with
a real spring in her step
an onlooker said. But
this morning, when I telephoned
myself, I said I didn't want to say
any more, as yet.

I Can Wait

Delete as appropriate

For the last train/plane/boat or bus,
for the last chance plan/lover or saloon,
for my/your last minute change of sex/
heart or mind. He/she/they/we can't/won't

sing/cook/dance or tell the time, but I
can hold on or off, hang about and on,
for the right/wrong time to call/go back/
find my creased/lost/void/no time barred/

expenses spared return. Can laugh/cry
question and plead—seize the platform/
world or stage, tap dance/torture tease
until the audience: enemies/friends/tinkers

tailors/soldiers/sailors laugh/cry/applaud
or get up and leave. Can wait in the light/
dark wings for the right/wrong second/
minute/to find my needle/thread/head/

keys or match, for you to catch my cold/
snow drift/madness/last train home.
Have my ticket/luggage/coffee/name/
unbearable/book/life/magazine. I'm waiting

for the right time to lose my rag/the plot/
my mind, to throw down/up or away my gauntlet/
breakfast/lunch and dinner/his/her home address/
photograph and number, to break your/my neck/

date or fate, to discard in this strange time/city/
world my atlas/A to Z/inaccurate map,
before you can say/understand or underline
a single word.

Children's Hour

An empty playground, a city park by night,
the shadow of swings—still—
their oil and grease out of sight.

We stood close at last, in the false glow
of neon light, shadows large against small rows
of houses and flats, our voices loud,

echoing along the streets under
London Bridge. Alone, I'd have hurried,
looked behind, and almost waited for

assault as expected as your lips, finally,
on mine, slow as the trains swerving above
our heads. Covered in a swarm,

a mass of jumpers, uniforms, red and pale blue
and grey, and knees, pink, brown
and black with grazes too small to see

and shouts loud but not loud enough
to hear, even with my face pressed
to the grime of the glass—a roundabout,

the swings and a seesaw. I see them
from the train at day, and remember how
abandoned and quiet, they once waited for dawn and flight.

If Winter Comes

— SHAKESPEARE, *The Winter's Tale*

The Tempest, Pericles, Cymbeline,
I keep reading how in those late plays,
self-knowledge is the key—*The Winter's Tale*:
that night when I found you out of the blue,
staring across the foyer, as I stared at you.

So we reached for each other, and touched: for this
long moment my arms wrapped around a statue,
warm and breathing and within my grasp,
friends, hovering, turning to ice creams
and programmes and drinks, slipping out of view.

*This evening's performance will recommence
in three minutes* . . . bells pronouncing my sense
of emergency, of fateful second chance,
wine to be drunk, hurriedly gulped down,
and more planned for later, *If you're about?*

And later after we clapped, alone, separately,
in the dark, and thronged in the crowd, apart,
I watched you slip away. Your skin I remember,
pale as a flame and as impossible to hold,
as unforgettable as that line that afterwards slid

for days like mercury in my veins, making my heart
hot, the pit of my stomach cold, how you rust,
how you rust through my glistering, and then
checking later, much later, *self-knowledge* at last
to find it should have been the other way around.

An Arrival

St Petersburg

No city lights or veins
of slow cars; no clustered
amber glow; no roads

or dark spaces without
houses; only black pines, mile
after mile—needles answering

someone else's footfall
easily as a sprung stage
or gymnast's mat—loaded

with heavy flakes, they nod
assent, resigned and soundless
as the plane lands in the snow.

Winter Palace

Thick flakes press
and die against the glass.
Hardheartedness
melts as fast.

In the private rooms
of the tsars,
thick flakes crash land
and disappear; gone

as soon as dusk:
the luminous blue
the banked up clouds,
briefly darken to—

bright and elemental
as blood on snow.
It feels like spilling more
to admit that it's not

the stale polish or dust
on the air, that has got
down my throat.
I stand at the window

thinking of one,
spoiled family, in their vast
cold house, pale and
breakable as dolls (porcelain,

sent from France,
with little silks and furs)
watching thick flakes press
and die against

the glass, or make
for the frozen river
or the huge silent square
I slowly head across.

Arabesque

I walked so far in boots on snow
the skin of my feet is yellow:
rough to the touch; hard packed

as ice, adamant as a lovebite.
They refuse, even now, back on
floor boards and tiles to soften or fade.

I hear myself move like the dulled clatter
of drummed fingers or *pointe* shoes
on wood. Mid-afternoon—in Russia

it would be dark. I open the window,
watch the steam escape and make a *banya*
of my luke warm bath. Weak and mild

as coffee and vodka and winter here,
I take a stone, try to chide my heels
back into soft pink shape—give up,

get out, and drip dry like a thaw
and still hear the blunt pebble clatter
as if at any second I'm going to arch

taut as a bridge across the frozen river
and wait, lit up, the way the hardened feet
of dancers wait, to almost fall, into the next beat.

The Understudy

chooses her moment
with a whisper
of a sore throat, a twisted

ankle, a tendon plucked
out of place
tenderly as a heavy stem.

The understudy chooses
a long night, with a hiss
you can't dismiss,

the radio left on,
persistence that stabs
like a piece of broken mirror.

Lucky for her,
with her blue blue eyes,
cold and bright

as the morning sky,
or stolen starling eggs . . .
Obvious, a stain of pollen

or yoke on your dress,
a stain that clings,
the way she does, levelly—

stretching herself
along the *barre*, she warms up too -
I'm fine, you mutter

as she unfurls a leg,
slow and delicate as a petal,
the flowers she'll send to you

tucked up in bed:
huge lilies, just in case
you think they're funereal,

just in case you feel
half-dead. *I'm fine*, you snap,
sudden as a broken stem,

or the thud on the mat
of letters and scripts, offers
of character parts,

voiceovers and crowd scenes,
loud as the crunch underfoot,
broken bottles

and fag ash on the floor,
the flute she tilted at you, her star
and bubbles rising . . . *Here's to us*,

she mouthed and admired her reflection
in your eyes, glassy and wet,
with fear of extinction.

Casablanca

My scarf's a gesture to vintage glamour.
Faded, fraying, I keep it close
around my neck, not quite by heart.

Versatile—carried like a favourite poem,
it gets translated, matched, like you
with any shade or hue. On a thousand

un-Arabian nights there are lights left on,
hoping with their dull, yellow glow
that you might show your face—

and perhaps you do. Content to follow
maybe you already know the way as well as me,
don't need to be told that mine is always

the familiar train and thought. Goodnight,
wherever it is you tread,
and if you have the heart or head for heights

I'm making ladder after ladder
piling each one up, a tower
of Babel on the desk . . . At the window

the sky is a flimsy paper set;
a po-faced moon hangs just below
black edged clouds, as if, reached for

it was about to fall then changed its mind.
Slung up there, thrown, casual
as an arm or scarf, a present

from Morocco, a place I haven't been,
a film I'd like to watch again. For now
this grainy fragile cloth will do, sure

one day to get lost or fall apart — till then
thin enough for souk and city heat,
midnight blue, thick enough

for frozen desert skies and altitude
and well suited, I like to think, to all
the hot cold stars I can't make out from here.

The Writer's Dairy
For my mother

On Amwell Street,
the dairy has been locked up,
abandoned carelessly,
as if an earthquake or volcano
exploded, and not just the decades,
and now all around, slow gentrification.

Damp years of junk mail
load the floor, cool as the milk
and the ice-cream which the signs
still promise can be carried away.
Wholesale boxes of chocolate bars
and crisps are balanced on the till—
brands and packets that till now
I'd never even noticed had disappeared.

Watched by her father,
a girl runs along the street,
he stands at the open door,
I don't know what it is I'm grieving for
or why I feel I should be finding out
who lives here now. It's only
second hand, that I know
the Pizza Express should be the toy shop
or that opposite the dairy, that delicatessen
was never there before.

In the window, the peering face
could almost be a child
who looked just like me,
who'd go in where now there are only
empties and unopened letters,
and dither and queue

and head off at a sprint, past the theatre
and the post office, to find the great grandmother
I never knew.

From St John's Street,
Rosebery Avenue, at dusk,
tiny lights—gold—caught in the trees.
I pass them all the time,
their insistent celebration,
and they always seem half right, just right,
and half all wrong
when on any given day,
I'm years too late for tea,
to stop and get the milk
and cream cakes on my way.

The sharp light dulls;
on the second autumnal day of the year
I take in a gaudy sunset:
pink and orange, bright
because not in spite of the dirt, spilling
beyond the grey, as far as where the city scatters
and someone somewhere still milks cows.

In the British Museum

Walk, don't run. A whirling crowd
are racing to Bolivia, Sri Lanka,
Papua New Guinea. Head left for Africa
and exit to Great Russell Street, right for Asia
and Montague Place, keep walking north
for India. In the Great Court watery blue
pours like a blessing, a mother holds her baby
up to the sky: laughs rippling over the scraps of cake
and sandwiches and abandoned
cappuccino cups. It's late, the cafe's sold out
and the galleries are closing one by one.
Kids' voices clatter: scattering worksheets
like ballot papers, cheeks flushed, they have run
for miles. In Room Twenty Three
I get the evil eye from the attendant who sighs
but lets me back through to what will be here
on any stolen rainy day. *Ehave*, a mask,
A thing of gladness, Papua New Guinea,
1932. In the photograph, sunlight, the sea held still,
and grins and sprints fixed, a crowd race
along the beach. Outside, another group
have been rounded up. Fat chestnuts pop
and fall into simple halves. I dawdle on the steps
and by the gates. *Walk, don't run . . .*
In the dusk, I head off along Great Russell Street,
start to fill in the blanks as best I can.

The Deep End

In the frieze, above the view
of the car park, the Athenian torch
is the size of the people, each shade of skin
in the Olympic rainbow scene
as unreal as the next. Below, slung, heavy bunting
separates the crocodiles marched in
to be taught to swim and the routine
of strokes and breaths that trail

in one another's wake. Cluttering up a lane,
I clear my head; the old man I always see
walks the middle stretch of each constitutional length.
The god swimmers, too,
are fading. A quarter mile or half
un-spools, and the time it takes
seems impossible to change, however
hard or fast you move towards the sign.

Thanksgiving

In the departure lounge, the sky
fades to dark. The colours are running away.
When the lights go down, I'm looking out
over the ice white wing, the arc of the land.
We fly past dawn — beside me
the guy who's carried on his whole case
watches Macy's parade on TV, and waits
sleepless, for his quick get away. We're almost there
before I'm awake, fixed to my tiny screen,
the channel with the blue sea and green land
and a red crayon seam to be sewn.
Skirting past St John, the furthest non-Alaskan tip,
hovering at thirty eight thousand feet
the cartoon plane is out of time, pulsing on.
Reappearing further than Lake Moosehead,
Timmins, Montreal, before dipping south — city
by city the eastern seaboard, Boston,
Providence, falls away off the map. Oslo,
London, Paris, Algiers flash back as if to say
Look how far we have come, look how easy it is to go.
Shut your eyes, with one finger choose where
and with who — this day should be gone,
a ghost of a time, but let down softly
to have another try, however close to the sun
we have flown, red-eyed and stiff-limbed
in the afternoon dusk, it almost sounds true.

Moon Man

Midtown—the hotel windows
are narrow eyes, taking in
the high skies and the bare brown brick,
early, before the day time haze,
the almost ice, precise glint of the glass;
November, already
the wind and the cars and the honking
near misses are chasing each other
down the avenues. The moon's a wink.

At every traffic light, the same man,
pale neon, white blue:
held together, so many dots joined up, elusive
and dependable, waited for; half his life's
a blank: a dark transformer board
above square digit fingers, a red hand raised,
a 'no' no one ignores, falling away to
day-glo pearls, an angel without wings,
gelatin silver, an almost friend . . .

Matins

The stars are tin-foil bright
as long as the offices are dark; through
sheaves of the *New York Times* I try to read
my way back down. It's all as watchable
as someone who never says
how long they'll stay. On a Monday

like any other, too cold for snow,
without me, nothing's changed. In the gym
the hotel shares, the pre-work work outs
will get going at five. Outside the library;
each head on a monolith paw,
the Aslan lions sleep on:

the fountains frozen, the park
pale with frost, my plane a trail of latte cloud *to go* . . .
Off their running machines, waking up,
they'll be walking to work—
the big eyed goddess of Starbucks cups
the only face tilted up at the sky.

Five Elements

Through pink and blue
stripes, inlaid, layers
of silver lights, building, where
open mouthed, the city used
to end with sky; so pink

and blue when it would suit
it better to be fire; dragon red
like the new year lanterns —
jelly fish floating — strung out
over dusk from Chinatown

to Oxford Street. Drive
west again. We could make
the sea: a boat and a drift
till land's a flicker. And later
if I dreamed, I'd dream

we got beyond the elements,
past every winter morning
I'll wake too soon; your face
a shadow, your shoulder turned:
just some solid shapes in a room,

studied, till dark's oyster grey —
as though its wooden bulges
and half light hollows might be
enough, to show me now
what state we're in.

The Writer

After The Writer, by Giancarlo Neri

I

How many first kisses
have these legs seen—by day,
only joggers and dogs move at speed.
Electric boats with paper sails
drift like talk. If you were mine,

barefoot, magnolia would be
soft grass and looking down
the trees' knotted vertebrae,
dandelion heads to blow away—
the rain, no more than fountain spray.

Where would the kids lie—
the boys with their skinny hips
and the girls in their jeans; where to,
for the man who's slept under here
every night for years or the one who wants,

once it's dark, again and again,
to write his name. If you were mine
the lazy footballers, who play as though
filmed and slowed down, would need
another goal. Soaring, the ball

thumps the desk's belly, its echo
loud as when, cat quiet, and full of other
lives, chasing ghosts from room to room,
leaping up, my knee hits wood—
sun burn tight on my face: one solid thing.

II

The whole place is shut down.
Out of season, through the night,
three tiny bulbs still gleam,
two orange, one pulsing green
like lights across a bay.

The air's heavy with a storm,
its first whispers that threaten half
to start, half to never come again.
Oblivious as a dreamer or a tide,
darkness rolls and, back turned, between

time zones, the chair's driftwood:
a raft with three lights left on,
sure I'll get up and sit, the words half blind,
running out, falling over themselves,
swimmers diving, on the line.

The Bedhead
After Calder

On the Canal, it has been light and quiet for hours.
Slapping at the sides of the house, the blue green
of cloudy glass, moves faster through the day
than, inside the dream palace half put up, half
falling down, the scene that plays again.

Below the cover, waking, a voice clear
as a cleaner, cooler river, says it's not as if *this*
and not just a picture or a piece can be
abandoned and begun again. Cold against
their skin, curled as easily as magnesium

twists in a chemistry set, steely as resolve,
knots like mercury—icing baubles
on a birthday cake—glimmer around the fish:
silver scales, half flying, half caught,
pinned down, and it's too bright to see

if it's just their scales, dazzling, or *them*
still more alive than dead, thrown—fluttering
in the sun on decks, or downstream from here,
the market stalls. His bedhead, her bed; the lovers
hooked: twisted in and out, of shape.

The Fall Project

The whole house taken over, big blooms
carried in, bigger maybe than from the florist
on the corner of Ladbroke Grove; more croissants,
eaten, standing around, than the *Buy Best* rip off store
could possibly pass off, shrivelling, as their own.
But maybe even they are coping—thriving—
on the cigarette demands; smoked into the small hours
in the shadows by the extras and runners, around
the lamp that makes a pool of 'evening' light
last well into the night ... All day with bottles of Evian,
the leads sit on the wall, in clothes that could be
vintage, from over the road, except, fifties-ish,
they look too new, like the house, which now
I come to think of it, they have been cleaning up,
whitening like teeth, all year. All year, to get to now,
the moment someone shouts *holding*:
and the grubby street falls still like one big pause,
long enough for something to *click* but only
in the movies when, really, it takes longer ...
And when it does ... I wake, still thinking of you
to find Woody Allen's moved in across the street,
making his latest, *untitled*, 'the fall project', making it up
as he goes along, freewheeling with trucks and cars
and florist and the van for dinner parked over
from where, behind the geraniums, I sit with coffee
and the papers. All day in yellow jackets
men worry, their brows like sums that don't add up,
trying to force days into long enough for a sweating couple
in a suit and gold trim skirt to say all there is to say,
just so. The sun's still burning when pale on blue,
for real, a full fat moon slides out. July will be August
by the time they're done. I mean, the light
and long nights, the summer will be gone.

Dress Not Taken

Carried off, into someone
else's life. Like all of the decades, they
float back again, as if, indolent as summer,
stock doesn't so much change as simply
drift. City sun, emptying papers,
days and squares. We won't have met or kissed
or done just yet. See the old green canopy,
chestnut umbrellas, the first fat black polka dots

of rain; then, windows in the trees, lanterns,
hustling, gently all night and tomorrow,
as though washed clean, all those
wrecked dresses shivering on the breeze
or maybe just shrugging free: 60s monochrome;
70s, ribbons, empire line—straps that could
break quick as this sharp snap of blue.
Let's leave it there, again, you know.

Cuba Libre

Sosua, Republica Dominicana

Huge jasmine flowers, bright white
as the clouds that hang around, high up,
as the sun goes down.
The gates of the hotel guarded, I slip through:
opposite, a liqueur store and empty paper rack.
Every day by nine or so, under a sign US PAPERS
the four or five copies of the *Miami Herald*
will have dwindled to one or none—Wednesday,
Monday's *Telegraph* is the closest thing to home.
The street's quiet. Vendors sit.
An old man man's the internet café,
high up MUSIC SHOP—*Communication Centre*
his sign, paint on tin, swings in the breeze.
He lays for hours flat out on the shop floor's cool,
at dusk, sits outside and gets up, now and then
to switch on one of the machines that groan
at the back of the room. I perch amidst piled up paintings—
large bad ones: sunsets, turbaned women
carry gaudy buckets; boys in shorts picking
unlikely looking fruit in English green fields,
flat as the one you see if you swim out
from the beach. Thin board: heavy air and amber
dusk streaked in colour, heavy palms that stoop
to dip in water held more still than here, the north side
of the island where Atlantic waves grow recklessly high,
and soar and crash over American and Canadian
college kids who bodyboard . . . or *boogyboard*.
It's all the same—surfing but lying down, possible
on more rum than any pirate ever drank: flying fish,
legs disappearing inside the waves, a cocktail mix
of Margarita salt and coconut oil on sunburned lips,
burned and half drowned on their Easter break.
Out there, with them, I twist my neck. We wait
and wait, for catastrophe: the big one, *it's brewing,*

it's brewing they yell, leaving me thinking ridiculously of tea,
caught up in wave after wave too strong to have taken on,
gasping, wanting that flat green field, a lime green crease
in the land where there might almost be a cricket
or a baseball game below the rough line of the hills,
charcoal jagged, remember, a rushed first draft;
the short fat clustered palms and few restaurant shacks,
the rocks to the west and the stretched arm
of the bay and to the east, the new beach
last year's storm threw down like a towel,
wanting all this to reappear as easily as, each night,
the lights of the next town. Crusted jewels—
yellow, green, blue—the whole washed up place so small
that there's nothing there all day suddenly
pinned down, glittering, like sequins on the costumes
of the carnival our bus trailed on the way here. Only now
those houses catch the light, like the sea, with its calm,
fooling pools of opal green. The stars are smudged,
their edges taken off by mist or spray from the waves
on a sky as dark as when time after time after
time the lights fail and the room, like all the rest,
plunges into darkness. The whole island gone
for a second that becomes five or six or ten
and surfacing again: flickering, hesitating
the way I do, out there, never sure I'll get up
and run back for more, out where anyone
could disappear with as little oily spirit trace
as ice in a drink, pulled down to nothingness,
reaching up to be let back through to the heavy air,
the beach, the streets and corrugated tin bars
that could crumple easily as cans; the paintings
nobody takes home tacked up in rows; the jasmine
and the empty paper racks, sold out,
with no news due for days.

Notes

THE WRITER'S DAIRY describes a real dairy, Lloyd's on Amwell Street in Islington. The idea for the poem came out of a typo in a letter asking me to keep a 'writer's dairy.'

FIVE ELEMENTS was a collaboration with the photographer Julian Bolt, for his 2006 show of that title at the Alexia Goethe Gallery. There's roughly a stanza of my poem for each of the Chinese elements (metal, fire, water, air and earth) that he photographed.

THE WRITER was commissioned by Rollo Contemporary Art, the UK gallery of the Italian sculptor Giancarlo Neri. Neri's sculpture, The Writer, a monumental desk and chair, was installed on Parliament Hill Fields for six months in 2005.

Before this the piece was for three years in the Park Ada, on the outskirts of Rome, where I first saw it. The artist, Giancarlo Neri, maintains that chairs are more interesting than writers, 'A chair for me is always the start of a story; it exists only because of a person. Someone has gone away or someone is coming back.'

Part II of the poem refers to some of his other works: in particular, Chairs at Sea, two huge floating chairs, in the Bay of Positano and 143 Lights in Capri, a path of chairs, each lit by a single bulb, which were installed on a disused coast road.

THE BEDHEAD imagines the relationship between the collector Peggy Guggenheim and the sculptor Alexander Calder. Calder's sculpture was used by Guggenheim on her bed long after the end of their affair and is still in the collection of her museum in Venice. A low single story building on the Grand Canal, it was built to house her and her collection. It was meant to be a five story palazzo but she ran out of money.